For my children, who taught me that
love grows in the smallest moments.

Love Grows Here

Copyright © 2026 Dean Menso
All rights reserved.

No part of this book may be reproduced, distributed, or transmitted in any form or by any means, including photocopying, recording, or other electronic or mechanical methods, without the prior written permission of the publisher, except in the case of brief quotations embodied in critical reviews and certain other noncommercial uses permitted by copyright law.

Publisher:
Truly Rooted Press

Contact:
hello@trulyrootedmedia.com
www.trulyrootedmedia.com

Illustrations by Rabia Batool

This is a work of fiction. Any resemblance to actual persons, living or dead, events, or places is purely coincidental.

ISBN: 979-8-9938969-1-5

First Edition

It starts in the soil, a family view— of where we came from, and all that we do.

We dig a small hole, a home for a hope, then tuck in a seed on a soft, earthy slope. The soil sticks under my fingernails, a tiny brown seed full of untold tales.

I poke at the dirt. "Is it growing yet?" I sigh and I slump and I start to fret. You smile and you whisper, "Patience, my dear. Good things take time for their magic to clear."

We pull out the mean stuff, the rough and the wild— the things that don't help the soft things inside. "Make room for the good," you always say, "Even strong flowers need space to play."

But not all trouble comes from the ground—a worm sneaks in without a sound. It nibbles a leaf, and you notice it there. You tell me a story as you show me your care. You say your first tomatoes were eaten by worms, and it took you a long time to learn the new terms. But you tried again.

Some days the sun hides, and storms roll through. The rain makes a puddle inside my shoe.

When the wind howls loud, you hold me tight, and we watch the garden in the grey afternoon light. You say the rain helps our little plant drink. It grows even stronger than we might think.

Then one morning I see it! A little green ball! So tiny and perfect, I let out a call! You laugh and you lift me so I can see,

THE VERY FIRST TOMATO, GROWN BY YOU AND ME!

The green ball gets bigger and starts to turn red. While we wait, happy stories fill up my head. You tell me about the mango tree you grew up climing. You said the best ones were at the very top, where you'd sit in the branches and eat them, barefoot, non-stop.

My sister tells our tomato stories each day— she says she's helping it grow that way. And you hum a tune while you prune the vine, the same one Oma hummed, you say it's a sign. You say she believed every garden, even when tired, was worth all the love that it ever required.

Today is the day! The fruit's red and deep. A promise the little green seedling did keep! We cook it together, just me and you, and remember the lesson you learned to be true. You tried and you tried, and now we know why— You grow the best tomatoes under the sky!

We're not just planting food— we're planting stories in the soil, memories in every leaf, and love in every root.

And even when the flowers fade, their roots hold tight below. And I know when you're gardening all alone, your love for Oma is clearly shown.

And you tell me that in every hue, A seed from Oma was planted by you. And all our love helps the garden grow, With every story and each new row.

And they'll hear the story, tried and true— of my Papa and Oma, and the garden our love grew.